SHRI RAM - |

THIS BOOK GIVES YOU A LITTLE KNOWLEDGE ABOUT PRABHU SHRI RAM

NAITIK ASTHANA

Copyright © Naitik Asthana
All Rights Reserved.

This book has been self-published with all reasonable efforts taken to make the material error-free by the author. No part of this book shall be used, reproduced in any manner whatsoever without written permission from the author, except in the case of brief quotations embodied in critical articles and reviews.

The Author of this book is solely responsible and liable for its content including but not limited to the views, representations, descriptions, statements, information, opinions and references ["Content"]. The Content of this book shall not constitute or be construed or deemed to reflect the opinion or expression of the Publisher or Editor. Neither the Publisher nor Editor endorse or approve the Content of this book or guarantee the reliability, accuracy or completeness of the Content published herein and do not make any representations or warranties of any kind, express or implied, including but not limited to the implied warranties of merchantability, fitness for a particular purpose. The Publisher and Editor shall not be liable whatsoever for any errors, omissions, whether such errors or omissions result from negligence, accident, or any other cause or claims for loss or damages of any kind, including without limitation, indirect or consequential loss or damage arising out of use, inability to use, or about the reliability, accuracy or sufficiency of the information contained in this book.

Made with ♥ on the Notion Press Platform
www.notionpress.com

Here, in this book you will get a bit more information of a sanatani god:

SHRI RAM

He was born in Ayodha, son of king Dasrath.

He have three mothers:

-Mata Kaushlaya

-Mata Sumitra

-Mata Kaikeyi

Contents

Foreword

They are four brothers :
- Shri Ram
- Shri Bharat
- Shri Laxman
- Shri Shatrughan

Preface

- Shri Ram was the son of Mata Kaushlaya.

   - Shri Bharat was the son of Mata Kaikeyi.

   - Shri Laxman and Shatrughan was the son of Mata Sumitra.

Acknowledgements

They have unbreakable love.
    But may be this is not accept to their fate.

Prologue

We would read about them all in different parts of my books.

xiii

-**HELLO ALL THERE THIS IS _NAITIK ASTHANA_ WRITING ABOUT A SANATANI GOD _SHRI RAM._**

- ENJOY THIS BY READING ABOUT HIM AND HIS ADVENTROUS LOVE.

CHAPTER ONE

SHRI RAM ON THIS EARTH

Let's start about king Dasrath:

- <u>**King dasrath was the son of king Aja of Kosala.**</u>

He was the 60th king in the solar dynasty he was born in Ayodhya. his son is King Dasrath.

King Dasrath was also born in Ayodhya, he was the 61th king of the solar dynasty he have three wives :

- Kaushlaya

- Sumitra

- Kaikeyi

After many time of marraige, not getting the son, the king worried and goes to a brahmin being a king of Ayodhya, and held a homa in their palace.

Then after a few time they got sons :

- Raja Ram from Mata Kaushlaya

- Shri Bharat from Mata Kaikeyi

- Shri Laxman and Shatrughan from Mata Sumitra.

After getting sons they got all happy and held a function in whole Ayodhya to celebrate the birth of their upcoming king and four prince'sof their dynasty.

Soon when all four kids become enough big, theking decided to send their children's to gurukul for getting the knowledge of percept and weapons in Indian language shashtra and sastra.

They all went to Gurukul and their teacher was Maharishi Vashisht, he taught them all the principles of life and all the knowledge from vedas. [OUR FOUR VEDAS : RIGVEDA, SAMAVEDA, YAJURVEDA, ATHARVAVEDA].

Shri Ram went to gurukul when he was 16 years old.

When they all came back from their gurukul, they stayed a few time more in his territory AYODHYA.

But, as I mentioned earlier this happiness in their all's life is not accepted to thir fate.

THIS IS NOT THE END OF THE STORY BUT I WILL PROCEED IT IN _SHRI RAM - ||_.

Shri Ram

<u>*IN THIS BOOK TILL NOW WE HAVE DONE READING ABOUT SHRI RAM AND W WILL ALSO DISCUSS ABOUT MORE CHAPTERS ABOUT HIS LIFE IN MY UPCOMING BOOKS.*</u>

<u>*-SHRI RAM - ||*</u>

<u>*AND MANY MORE ABOUT ANOTHER POPULAR SANATANI GOD*</u>

<u>*-PRABHU SHRI KRISHANA*</u>

www.ingramcontent.com/pod-product-compliance
Lightning Source LLC
Chambersburg PA
CBHW022048150726
47990CB00004B/1655